TRIANGLE HISTORIES
THE CIVIL WAR

JAMES LONGSTREET

Melanie LeTourneau

BLACKBIRCH PRESS

THOMSON
———★———
GALE

Detroit • New York • San Diego • San Francisco
Boston • New Haven, Conn. • Waterville, Maine
London • Munich

Published by Blackbirch Press
10911 Technology Place
San Diego, CA 92127
Web site: http://www.galegroup.com/blackbirch
e-mail: customerservice@galegroup.com

Printed in China

10 9 8 7 6 5 4 3 2 1

Photo credits:
Cover, pages 10, 12, 17, 18, 20, 21, 28, 39, 44, 46, 53, 55, 74, 78, 94, 98,
100 © Dover Publications; cover, backcover, pages 4, 14, 22, 24, 32, 34, 41,
47, 59, 71, 76, 82 © North Wind Picture Archive; pages 16, 26, 29, 50, 52,
57, 66, 73, 86, 90 © The Library of Congress; pages 36, 37, 63, 68, 84, 92
© National Archives.

Library of Congress Cataloging-in-Publication Data
Le Tourneau, Melanie.
James Longstreet 1 by Melanie Le Tourneau.
          p. cm. — (The Civil War)
Includes index.
Summary: Discusses the life and career of James Longstreet, Confederate
general and trusted adviser to Robert E. Lee.
          ISBN 1-56711-564-0 (hardcover: alk. paper)
1. Longstreet, James, 1821-1904—Juvenile literature. 2. Generals—
Confederate States of America—Biography—Juvenile literature.
3. Confederate States of America. Army—Biography—Juvenile literature.
4. United States—History—Civil War, 1861-1865—Campaigns—Juvenile
literature. [1. Longstreet, James, 1821-1904—Juvenile literature. 2. Generals.
3. Confederate States of America. 4. United States—History—Civil War,
1861-1865.1 1. Title. 11. Civil War (Blackbirch Press)
E467.1155 L47 2002
973.7'3'092—dc   212001005813

CONTENTS

PREFACE: THE CIVIL WAR

Nearly 150 years after the final shots were fired, the Civil War remains one of the key events in U. S. history. The enormous loss of life alone makes it tragically unique: More Americans died in Civil War battles than in all other American wars combined. More Americans fell at the Battle of Gettysburg than during any battle in American military history. And, in one day at the Battle of Antietam, more Americans were killed and wounded than in any other day in American history.

Slaves did the backbreaking work on Southern plantations.

As tragic as the loss of life was, however, it is the principles over which the war was fought that make it uniquely American. Those beliefs—equality and freedom—are the foundation of American democracy, our basic rights. It was the bitter disagreement about the exact nature of those rights that drove our nation to its bloodiest war.

The disagreements grew in part from the differing economies of the North and South. The warm climate and wide-open areas of the Southern states were ideal for an economy based on agriculture. In the first half of the 19th century, the main cash crop was cotton, grown on large farms called plantations. Slaves, who were brought to the United States from Africa, were forced to do the backbreaking work of planting and harvesting cotton. They also provided the other labor necessary to keep plantations running. Slaves were bought and sold like property, and had been critical to the Southern economy since the first Africans came to America in 1619.

The suffering of African Americans under slavery is one of the great tragedies in American history. And the debate over whether the United States government had the right to forbid slavery—in both Southern states and in new territories—was a dispute that overshadowed the first 80 years of our history.

For many Northerners, the question of slavery was one of morality and not economics. Because the Northern economy was based on manufacturing rather than agriculture, there was little need for slave labor. The primary economic need of Northern states was a protective tax known as a tariff that would make imported goods more expensive than goods made in the North. Tariffs forced Southerners to buy Northern goods and made them economically dependent on the North, a fact that led to deep resentment among Southerners.

Economic control did not matter to the anti-slavery Northerners known as abolitionists. Their conflict with the South was over slavery. The idea that the federal government could outlaw slavery was perfectly reasonable. After all, abolitionists contended, our nation was founded on the idea that all people are created equal. How could slavery exist in such a country?

For the Southern states that joined the Confederacy, the freedom from unfair taxation and the right to make their

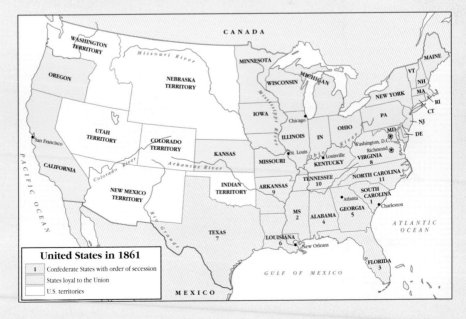

own decisions about slavery was as important a principle as equality. For most Southerners, the right of states to decide what is best for its citizens was the most important principle guaranteed in the Constitution.

The conflict over these principles generated sparks throughout the decades leading up to the Civil War. The importance of keeping an equal number of slave and free states in the Union became critical to Southern lawmakers in Congress in those years. In 1820, when Maine and Missouri sought admission to the Union, the question was settled by the Missouri Compromise: Maine was admitted as a free state, Missouri as a slave state, thus maintaining a balance in Congress. The compromise stated that all future territories north of the southern boundary of Missouri would enter the Union as free states, those south of it would be slave states.

In 1854, however, the Kansas-Nebraska Act set the stage for the Civil War. That act repealed the Missouri Compromise and by declaring that the question of slavery should be decided by residents of the territory, set off a rush of pro- and anti-slavery settlers to the new land. Violence between the two sides began almost immediately and soon "Bleeding Kansas" became a tragic chapter in our nation's story.

With Lincoln's election on an anti-slavery platform in 1860, the disagreement over the power of the federal government reached its breaking point. In early 1861, South Carolina became the first state to secede from the Union, followed by Mississippi, Florida, Alabama, Georgia, Louisiana, Virginia, Texas, North Carolina, Tennessee, and Arkansas. Those eleven states became the Confederate States of America. Confederate troops fired the first shots of the Civil War at Fort Sumter, South Carolina, on April 12, 1861. Those shots began a four-year war in which thousands of Americans—Northerners and Southerners—would give, in President Lincoln's words, "the last full measure of devotion."

OPPOSITE: The Confederate attack on Fort Sumter began the Civil War.

Introduction:
"The Saddest Day
of My Life"

During June and early July 1863, General Robert E. Lee marched his Army of Northern Virginia up the Shenandoah Valley. Outside the farming town of Gettysburg, Pennsylvania, Rebels forced their way into Union territory. The Union Army of the Potomac fought desperately to hold off the advancing enemy troops.

On the evening following the second day's fighting, Lee met with General James Longstreet, his most trusted advisor. Lee was determined to make one final massive assault that would crush the enemy resistance, and he explained his plan to Longstreet. From their base at Seminary Ridge, Confederate infantry would cross nearly a mile of open land to attack Union forces dug in on Cemetery Ridge.

Longstreet listened with alarm to the plan. The enemy would be expecting the attack, he protested. It would not be a charge, it would be suicide.

Lee dismissed Longstreet's objections. "No," he insisted. "The enemy is there, and I am going to strike him." Lee ordered Longstreet to have General George Pickett's division lead the attack.

On July 3, Longstreet blasted the Union army with more than 100 artillery pieces. Longstreet hoped the artillery bombardment would disrupt Union lines and give Pickett's men at least a small

8

More than two-thirds of the Confederate forces led by George Pickett were killed at the Battle of Gettysburg.

chance of success. Unknown to the Rebels, however, the artillery fire sailed over the target. Union troops remained unharmed behind a stone wall.

Finally, Pickett approached Longstreet and asked, "Shall I advance?" Longstreet nodded.

With quick steps and grim faces the young men moved forward. Suddenly, the Union cannons exploded in a deafening roar. Shot and shell cut Pickett's men to ribbons. Non-exploding cannon-balls rolled through the Rebel lines and took down dozens at a time.

Though some Rebels reached the wall, Union fire finally turned them back. "When the smoke cleared," Longstreet later recalled, "Pickett's division was gone."

Less than half an hour after the attack began, nearly two-thirds of Pickett's men lay dead. Lee's plan had failed, and the Battle of Gettysburg was lost. "That day," Longstreet said years later, "was the saddest of my life."

9

Chapter 1

A s one of the three main commanders of the Army of Northern Virginia, General James Longstreet led Confederate troops in some of the bloodiest battles of the Civil War, from Manassas in 1861 to Appomattox Court House in 1865. Yet his contributions to the Rebel cause are often overshadowed by those of the other two commanders, legends Robert E. Lee and Thomas "Stonewall" Jackson.

OPPOSITE: James Longstreet participated in most of the major Civil War battles.

Although Longstreet spent most of the war in Virginia, he had never lived in that state before the war erupted. Unlike Lee and Jackson, Virginia natives who had spent little if any time in the Deep South before the war's outbreak, Longstreet had grown up in South Carolina, Georgia, and Alabama. He had also served as a United States Army officer in Louisiana, Florida, and Texas.

James Longstreet was born in South Carolina. In anticipation of the birth of her fifth child, his mother traveled from the family farm in Georgia to stay with her mother-in-law at the Longstreet family's cotton plantation. When the boy was born on January 8, 1821, he was named James after his father. A few weeks later, his mother returned to Georgia with her new son.

On his mother's side, the young child's ancestors included William the Conqueror, who centuries before had vanquished all of England. James was also a relative of John Marshall—the first Chief Justice of the Supreme Court, who had fought to strengthen the power of the federal courts.

John Marshall was the first Chief Justice of the Supreme Court and one of Longstreet's relatives.

James spent the first nine years of his life in Gainesville, Georgia, which edged a rugged frontier. As a young boy, James followed his older brother, William, and his sister, Anna, through the Southern wilderness. Together, they spent the days swimming, hunting, fishing, and riding horses. These activities strengthened James's physical endurance and determination. His father noted the boy's sturdy build and resolute character and nicknamed him "Old Pete," after the Biblical disciple whose name meant "rock."

In 1828, Andrew Jackson defeated John Quincy Adams in the U.S. presidential election.

As he read stories of Caesar, Napoleon, and George Washington, young James imagined becoming a soldier. His father hoped that James would one day attend the famous military academy of West Point. It was the only way that an education would be attainable. The Longstreet family had grown to nine children, and the family farm was not one that provided great wealth.

Gaining admittance to the academy, however, would not be easy. Although James came from a well-known Southern family, appointments to West Point were hard to obtain. James's father knew his son was only an average student. Gaining an appointment to the finest military academy post in the nation would take more than just family connections.

In order to improve his son's chances and his education, James's father arranged for James to live with his brother, Augustus Longstreet, a well-respected attorney. As his head filled with dreams of military glory, James moved to Augusta, Georgia, to live with his aunt and uncle. There, James attended a nearby prep school, which he hoped would prepare him for West Point.

13

Three years later, while James was pursuing his studies, his father died of cholera. His wife was left to care for the children. Mary Longstreet decided to move her family to northern Alabama. James, however, stayed with his aunt and uncle, who treated him as their own son. James never forgot their warmth and kindness. Indeed, Longstreet credited his uncle Augustus with helping to shape him into the man he became.

A Southern Way of Life

From the time he was a young boy, James had been surrounded by slavery. On his uncle's plantation, he witnessed the backbreaking labor expected of slaves. To him, slavery was a normal part of everyday life. And though he was friendly with the slaves on the Longstreet plantation, he did not question their oppression.

Slaves at work in the fields on a southern plantation.

The person who had the most influence on James's ideas about slavery and other issues of the day was his uncle. Augustus was a popular writer, lawyer, and speaker, and one of the South's most outspoken supporters of state's rights. At that time, there was strong support for the principle of "nullification" among leading politicians in the South. That principle, introduced by Senator John C. Calhoun of South Carolina, stated that if a state's citizens disagreed with a law passed by the federal government, they could vote to nullify—ignore—the legislation. This concept was bitterly opposed by many Northern lawmakers and became one of the first dividing lines between North and South.

★ In 1833, Lucretia Mott helped to organize the Female Anti-Slavery Society in Philadelphia. ★

As a young boy, James did not concern himself with political beliefs such as state's rights or nullification. On the other hand, because he admired his uncle so much, he adopted these beliefs as he grew up.

West Point Bound

Longstreet's dreams of West Point had not died with his father. With the help of his Uncle Augustus, Longstreet received an appointment from Alabama to join the academy as a cadet in the freshman class of 1838. Among the well-known Southerners who recommended James for West Point was John C. Calhoun himself, the champion of nullification.

15

Life in the North was shockingly different from anything Longstreet had known on the Southern frontier. Gone were the days of warmth and adventure. Now, at the young age of 17, he was left to take care of himself in the frigid, gloomy winters of the Northeast.

Although West Point was operated by the U.S. military, cadets were trained more in academics than in hand-to-hand combat. Longstreet studied mathematics and physics, and struggled as much with his schoolwork as with life in a strange part of the country. He had spent his childhood exploring the hot Southern wilderness, not bent over books. By his own admission, the young

Longstreet attended the U.S. Military Academy at West Point, New York. This illustration shows the academy in the early 1800s.

cadet "had more interest in the school of the soldier, horsemanship, sword exercise, and the outside game of foot-ball than in academic classes."

At well over 200 pounds, Longstreet was a large and robust young man, and popular among his classmates. Rugged and outspoken, he was the opposite of one of his closest friends, the modest and slight Ulysses S. Grant. The two young men, however, did share a great love for horsemanship. Longstreet was fond of pranks, and during his time at West Point, he accumulated demerits for such offenses as "spitting," "long hair," and "disturbance during study hours." In 1842, when he graduated, he ranked fifty-fourth out of a class of 62 graduates. His military career was about to begin.

Ulysses S. Grant was a good friend of Longstreet's at West Point.

Chapter 2

"THE SOLDIER'S LIFE"

After graduation in 1842, Longstreet was stationed in the 4th Infantry in St. Louis, Missouri, where Lieutenant Colonel John Garland was second in command. There, Longstreet became infatuated with the colonel's daughter, Maria Louise Garland. From then on, the young soldier always carried a photograph of young Miss Garland with him.

OPPOSITE: James Longstreet first saw military action during the Mexican-American War.

Julia Dent, Longstreet's cousin, married Ulysses S. Grant.

The following year, his friend Grant, who had just graduated near the bottom of his own class at West Point, arrived in St. Louis. Longstreet recalled Grant's "noble . . . generous heart" and "lovable character," and the men immediately renewed their friendship. Longstreet even decided to introduce Grant to his cousin, Miss Julia Dent.

Grant, who wore the shoulder bars of a lieutenant, was teased by Miss Dent's other suitors as "the small man with the large epaulets." Four years later, however, Grant was the suitor Miss Dent chose to marry, and Longstreet was in the wedding party.

War with Mexico

In May 1844, Longstreet was sent to Louisiana to join the troops known as "The Army of Observation." In March 1845, he was assigned as lieutenant in the Eighth Regiment and joined his company in St. Augustine, Florida. Much of his service consisted of setting up posts to protect settlers. For the most part, the work was boring and inactive.

"The soldier's life in those days was not encouraging," Longstreet later wrote of that time. He also realized, however, that "influences were then at work that were beginning to brighten the horizon."

By "influences," Longstreet meant that there was a strong likelihood the U.S. would go to war with Mexico in a long-standing dispute over the southern border of the new state of Texas. Texas had declared independence from Mexico in 1838, yet Mexico still considered Texas a rebellious province.

In the rapidly expanding United States, many Americans wanted to annex, or add, Texas to the United States of America. They believed in "Manifest Destiny," the idea that the fate of the United States was to expand from ocean to ocean, across all of North America. When Democrat James K. Polk, a supporter of Manifest Destiny, was elected to the presidency of the United States in 1844, the Texas question was all but decided. On July 4, 1845, Texas became a state. Mexico viewed the action as a declaration of war, and the following year, fighting broke out between the two nations.

★

The Narrative of the Life of Frederick Douglass was published in the spring of 1845.

★

James K. Polk was elected president in 1844.

Longstreet thought of the war as an event to "brighten the horizon" because he had decided to follow a military career. For him, war was the best chance to rise through the ranks.

Longstreet participated in eight conflicts of the war, including one of its most famous battles.

21

Longstreet was injured during the Battle of Chapultepec, one of the last battles of the Mexican-American War.

Major General Winfield Scott led the United States army in an attack on Mexico City, the Mexican capital. On a hill near Mexico City, a towering fortress called the Castle of Chapultepec stood as a final defense to the city.

As Scott's men approached the castle, they were blasted by cannon fire. Longstreet, carrying the regimental flag, fought bravely toward the fortress. Suddenly, he stumbled as a musket ball tore through his leg. As he fell to the ground, Longstreet refused to let the flag fall, and instead passed the regimental colors to his friend George Pickett. When Pickett triumphantly climbed over the wall of Chapultepec, he was still carrying the flag.

Afterward, Longstreet stayed in Mexico until his severe wound had healed enough to allow him to make the difficult journey home. Longstreet recovered with remarkable speed. He returned home soon after the war's end in 1848, eager to see Maria Louise Garland. On March 8, the two were married.

At the war's end, settlers poured into the enormous state of Texas, thereby displacing thousands of Mexicans and American Indians. In addition to Texas, the United States gained from Mexico the land that would become California, Arizona, Nevada, New Mexico, Utah, and part of Colorado. The young nation had also gained a generation of combat-tested soldiers. Among these battle-hardened veterans were Ulysses Grant, Thomas "Stonewall" Jackson, and Jefferson Davis. Perhaps the most well-known Mexican War veteran was Robert E. Lee, whom Winfield Scott called the "finest soldier I have ever seen in the field."

Fighting on the Frontier

In the fall of 1848, Longstreet returned to Louisiana. There, he fought numerous battles with Native Americans, who resisted as more Americans moved onto their lands. In 1849, he was sent to San Antonio, Texas, where the army's role again was to protect settlements and immigrants. For the next year and a half, Longstreet gained the

23

important experience of commanding an army post.

As his career on the frontier continued, Longstreet spent three years on the U.S.-Mexican border in El Paso, Texas. His wife and two boys stayed 600 miles east in San Antonio, where a third son was born in 1853. The infant became ill and died the next year.

Eventually, Longstreet rose to the command of Fort Bliss, near El Paso, a position he held until 1858. Meanwhile, the Longstreet family continued to grow. A fourth child and first daughter was born in 1856 but lived only five months. The fifth child was born in 1857. As the children grew up on the rugged frontier, Longstreet and his wife wanted to be sure they received a good education.

While Longstreet was stationed in El Paso, Texas, his wife and children lived in San Antonio (pictured).

Because better schools existed in the East, Longstreet wrote his superiors in Washington to request duty in Pennsylvania, saying that 16 years of frontier service was long enough for any soldier.

Instead of an assignment back East, however, Longstreet received a six-month leave. First, he visited his uncle, who had become president of the College of South Carolina in Columbia. Longstreet then traveled north to enroll his two oldest sons in a prep school in Yonkers, New York. Finally, Longstreet reported for duty at Fort Leavenworth, Kansas. There he served for a year before being transferred to his father-in-law's command in Albuquerque, New Mexico. But that period of military life soon ended, as the nation moved to the brink of civil war.

In 1859, abolitionist John Brown was captured and hanged for leading a raid on the Harpers Ferry armory.

Chapter 3

THE ROAD TO WAR

The Civil War was rooted in conflicts that were as old as the nation itself. Even before the final shots of the Revolutionary War were fired, the country's founders feared that another great battle would soon erupt—a battle over the very principles on which the nation had been founded.

It was deeply ironic, most realized, that a nation whose own Declaration of Independence stated that "all men are created equal" had in large measure been built with the unpaid labor of millions of African slaves. Abolitionists—those who worked to end slavery—often referred to the principles of freedom set forth in the declaration to support their demand that slavery be brought to an end.

OPPOSITE: Fort Sumter, South Carolina. It was here that the Civil War began on April 12, 1861.

In another irony, the young nation's rules for self-government—the Constitution—which was written 11 years after the Declaration of Independence, regarded slaves as property and counted each slave as three-fifths of a person. The Constitution also gave to states all rights not assumed by the federal government. To many people, this meant that the Constitution allowed slavery, and that a state had the right to pass laws that permitted slavery to flourish.

Disagreements over states' rights and slavery grew in the first half of the nineteenth century, disagreements that led Abraham Lincoln to observe in a famous speech in 1859, "A house divided against itself cannot stand." He was right, and with his election as president in 1860, the structure of the Union began to collapse.

In December 1860, South Carolina became the first state to secede from the Union. By April 1861, ten other states had followed. On April 12, Confederate gunners fired the first shots of the Civil War at Fort Sumter, situated in the harbor of Charleston, South Carolina.

Abraham Lincoln

The carnage that consumed the nation for the next four years surpassed Americans' worst nightmares. Southern leaders knew that they had fewer

28

men and scantier resources than the North. To win the war, the Rebels would have to rely on their fighting ability, courage, and the superior skills of their commanding officers.

Farewell to the Union Army

As tensions rose, many West Point graduates of Southern origin rushed to join the Confederate army. Longstreet, however, moved slowly. He was actually planning to leave a military career behind in order to be closer to his wife and children. The

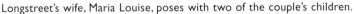
Longstreet's wife, Maria Louise, poses with two of the couple's children.

★

In August 1861,
Ulysses S. Grant was
promoted to the
rank of brigadier
general.

★

death of his own father when he was still a
young boy had made Longstreet a particu-
larly devoted family man. Now, at age 40,
Longstreet believed his fighting days were
through.

Longstreet also reacted slowly to
unfolding events because he was still a
federal soldier. Since his graduation from West
Point almost 20 years earlier, he had served the
United States. Although Longstreet did not want
the Southern states to leave the Union, he knew
that if the South broke away he would side with
it. Longstreet remembered his favorite uncle's
unshakable belief in states' rights, and he could
not oppose his family.

As his home states—Alabama, Georgia, and
South Carolina—seceded from the Union,
Longstreet left the Union army in June 1861 to
join the Confederacy. "It was a sad day when we
took leave of lifetime comrades and gave up
service of twenty years," Longstreet recalled.

As he said farewell to Union officers, many of
his longtime friends asked Longstreet to stay and
fight for the Union. After one Union captain
pleaded with Longstreet not to join the South,
"Old Pete" asked the man what he would do if his
state has seceded and called him to serve. The
captain replied to Longstreet, understandingly,
that he too would "obey the call."

Longstreet first tried to get an officer's commission
from Alabama, the state that had given him his

appointment to West Point. When nothing came of this request, Longstreet made his way to Richmond, Virginia, the capital of the Confederacy, located just 100 miles south of the Union capital in Washington, D.C.

While on his long journey across the South, Longstreet met an "intelligent and clever Texan," who rode with him to Virginia. The man, T.J. Goree, went on to serve as Longstreet's chief aide from the Battle of Bull Run until the end of the war.

No one doubted that violence between the North and the South was rapidly approaching. The extent to which that violence would engulf the nation, however, was unknown in 1861. President Lincoln believed that aside from a small group of Rebels, most Southerners were loyal to the Union. If war broke out, reasoned Lincoln, most Southerners would side with the North. Fighting would end, he believed, after a few short battles, in perhaps six months at most.

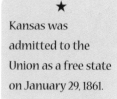

Kansas was admitted to the Union as a free state on January 29, 1861.

Lincoln could not have been more mistaken about the will of the South. In many ways, the states of the Confederacy were more unified in national spirit, and had more in common, than the 22 states of the North, which ranged from industrial Northeastern states to agricultural Midwestern states. Southerners such as Robert E. Lee often referred to their home states as "my country."

31

Richmond, Virginia, was the capital of the Confederacy. Longstreet arrived there in June 1861 and asked to be assigned as a paymaster in the Confederate army.

As Longstreet rode toward Richmond, he noticed that the Southern fighting spirit seemed to be everywhere. Years later he wrote of that time, "All was enthusiasm and excitement, and songs of 'Dixie and the South' were borne upon the balmy air."

On June 29, 1861, Longstreet arrived in Richmond. Unlike his West Point comrades who had resigned from the Union army to join the Confederacy, however, Longstreet did not want to fight—he thought he was too old. When he reached Virginia, he asked to be assigned as a paymaster.

At a time when the South needed all the experienced help it could find, Longstreet's request was out of the question. The South needed seasoned soldiers, and it needed them immediately. Confederate President Jefferson Davis refused to waste the skills of a West Point graduate on accounting. The president quickly promoted Longstreet to brigadier general and ordered him to take command of an infantry brigade at Manassas, Virginia, a railroad town midway between the two enemy capitals. "Old Pete's" long march from the first battle of the Civil War until the last was about to begin.

Among the men who became legends among Southern troops, only Lee and Jackson are more well known than Longstreet. Yet at the outbreak of the war, Jackson was a college professor in charge of training student volunteers. Lee was also far from battle, training volunteers in western Virginia. He did not become an important part of the Southern effort until mid-1862. Only Longstreet was in battle for all four years of the Civil War.

Chapter 4

Led by Union commander Irvin McDowell, the Union army marched more than thirty miles to Manassas, Virginia, in the first weeks of July 1861. Longstreet himself took a train from Richmond to Manassas. Here, near the Bull Run River, the Battle of Bull Run demonstrated the first horrors of the terrible war to come.

OPPOSITE: A Confederate sharpshooter takes aim from his perch in a tree.

35

Soldiers rest at Blackburn's Ford, where Longstreet and his men prevented Union forces from crossing the river.

The Battle of Bull Run

Although he was engaged only in the outskirts of the battle, it was obvious that Longstreet was a natural soldier. Assigned to guard the crossing of the river at a location known as Blackburn's Ford, his men prevented the Union army not only from crossing the river but also from mounting a flank attack on the main Rebel force under P. G. T. Beauregard. "Part of my line broke and started to run," Longstreet said of the battle in later years. "To stop the alarm I rode with sabre in hand for the leading files, determined to give them all that was in the sword and my horse's heels, or stop the break."

During this battle, Confederate general Thomas Jackson earned his famous nickname "Stonewall," for his corps' firm defensive stand on the area known as Henry Hill. After a daylong battle in blistering heat, the Rebels crushed the Union army. Federal troops broke from the battlefield and rushed in panic all the way back to Washington, D.C. Southern papers tauntingly referred to the retreat as "The Great Skedaddle."

Thomas "Stonewall" Jackson earned his nickname at the Battle of Bull Run.

Despite the taunts, however, both sides realized that this would be no rapid war. In the North, there was shock at the carnage, and grim determination to teach the Rebels a lesson in return. In the South, there was elation at the victory and optimism that the Rebel cause would win out. By the end of the battle, Longstreet's doubts about being too old for combat had faded.

In the months that followed, Longstreet proved himself a skillful soldier. He was strong and needed little sleep or food. Perhaps because of his massive strength and endurance, Longstreet rarely got sick and when he did, he recovered quickly.

The Rebel army was in high spirits during the fall of 1861—and General Longstreet was often at the center of celebrations. In a banquet following

37

Longstreet's promotion to major general, General Earl Van Dorn, one of Longstreet's West Point classmates, burst out singing what he believed should be the new Confederate anthem.

"Up on the table and show yourself," Longstreet joked. "We can't see you!"

To this Van Dorn had replied, "Not unless you stand by me." Longstreet happily climbed up the table with his classmate and began singing, "Let the words Country, Victory, and Honor awaken terror in the enemy. . . . It is a fine thing to face death crying, 'Freedom'!"

The time from April to December of 1861 seemed almost carefree for Confederate troops—and for Longstreet, too. Longstreet did not have Jackson's quick wit and intensity. Nor did he have Lee's dashing elegance. Even so, a volunteer from Georgia described him as being "a most striking figure . . . a soldier every inch, and very handsome, tall and well proportioned. General Longstreet is one of the kindest, best-hearted men I have ever known."

A Family Tragedy

In the second year of the war, 1862, the time of carefree spirit and optimism came to an end for both the South and for Longstreet. In January, an outbreak of scarlet fever swept through Richmond, where Longstreet's family lived. Longstreet rushed home after he received an urgent message from

38

his wife, only to find he was too late to help three of his children. In one week, his daughter, Mary Anne, and his sons Augustus Baldwin and James had died from the fever. Only the eldest, John Garland, had survived.

Longstreet and his wife were grief-stricken. Longstreet's friend George Pickett and his wife helped plan the funerals. Longstreet never described his grief in writing, but his friends noticed a change in him. Already a man of few words, he now became virtually silent. Men who expected to hear little from him to begin with became used to one-word answers. Longstreet stopped drinking whiskey and playing poker. "Old Pete" even refused to curse. He turned to the church and became devoutly religious.

Shiloh

Confederate general Albert Sidney Johnston helped launch a surprise attack on Grant at Shiloh.

While Longstreet was grieving, his old friend, Ulysses Grant, was fighting in Tennessee. Like Longstreet, Grant was a tenacious, determined soldier. After Grant had led two important Union victories, however, he nearly lost the first major battle in the western theater of the war.

In April 1862, Confederate generals Albert Sidney Johnston

39

On April 11, 1862, Union forces took control of Fort Pulaski in Georgia, giving Union soldiers upriver access to the Savannah River.

★

and P. G. T. Beauregard launched a surprise attack on Grant. His forces had crossed the Tennessee River at Pittsburg Landing and were on their way to seize the Confederacy's most important railroad junction. That junction, several miles south at Corinth, Mississippi, was the point at which the Memphis & Charleston railroad crossed the Mobile & Ohio Railroad. From that point, Southern troops could reach almost any region of the South by rail. To protect the junction, nearly 55,000 Rebel soldiers converged on Grant's army in a battle that took its name, Shiloh, from a church on the battlefield.

The Confederates were determined to drive the Union army away from their critical high ground back across the Tennessee River. And they very nearly did with their initial assault. After hours of brutal fighting in a dense oak thicket that came to be known as the "Hornet's Nest," the Rebels had pushed the Union army towards the river. Grant, however, was able to gather his artillery on an area of high ground and, with stiff-necked determination, drive the Rebels back. Instead of a defeat, the Union forces had their first victory in the West.

In the process, the Union suffered 13,047 casualties, while the Confederates suffered 10,694, including General Albert Sidney Johnston, who was killed by a stray bullet. By the end of April, it

The "Hornet's Nest" was the scene of brutal fighting at Shiloh.

had become clear to both sides that the misery and death would only become worse. All hope for a short war was lost.

Grant was soundly criticized for losing so many troops at Shiloh. And the battle had helped him realize that the course of the war had to be altered. "I gave up all idea of saving the Union except by complete conquest," Grant said after the fighting. True to this belief, the Union army began to destroy Confederate horses, cattle, food supplies, and crops.

★
In June 1862,
Congress passed
a law forbidding
slavery in federal
territories, but not
in states.
★

The Battle of Williamsburg

Although Longstreet was filled with grief over the deaths of his children, he remained fearless and savage on the battlefield. In early May 1862, Union General George B. McClellan and his huge Army of the Potomac embarked on the Peninsular Campaign. McClellan intended to take control of the peninsula bordered by the James and York rivers, then move northwest to attack Richmond.

Greatly outnumbered, Confederate General Joseph Johnston's men struggled to retreat through deep mud brought on by spring rains. In what became known as the Battle of Williamsburg, Longstreet—in command of 9,000 men—held Union troops off until Johnston's men could retreat. Late in the battle, Johnston joined Longstreet at the battle line. Longstreet had had few experiences commanding large forces, so Johnston was amazed to find that Longstreet, with his "clear head and brave heart," had the battle under control.

Lee Takes Charge

Late that month, however, during the same campaign against McClellan, Longstreet made a rare mistake. The Union army had been separated by the overflow of a river just ten miles away from Richmond, and Johnston moved in to attack one of the forces that had separated from the

Federal Battery awaits action during Peninsular Campaign.

main force. After some confusion, Longstreet led his troops down the wrong route. His attack of the enemy was further south than Johnston had planned. During the brisk fighting, Johnston was wounded. Robert E. Lee became the new commander of the Confederate army.

Less than a month after he took command, Lee faced a crisis in defending the Confederate capital of Richmond. McClellan had led his Union army within range of Richmond and was preparing to seize the city. McClellan's army consisted of more than 150,000 men and, unlike the tattered and

43

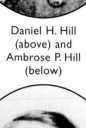

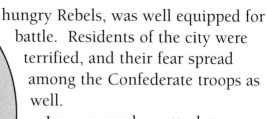

Daniel H. Hill (above) and Ambrose P. Hill (below)

hungry Rebels, was well equipped for battle. Residents of the city were terrified, and their fear spread among the Confederate troops as well.

Lee arranged an attack to force the Union army away from Richmond. The assault was to be led by Stonewall Jackson and supported by Generals Longstreet, Daniel H. Hill, and Ambrose P. Hill. On the day of the attack, however, Jackson was several hours late. A.P. Hill decided to move forward without Jackson, and his men were pummeled. Although Lee sent Longstreet and D.H. Hill to support the attack, the Union army held. Finally, when word of Jackson's arrival reached the Union army, they retreated for the night. Stonewall Jackson's battlefield reputation was such that his name alone was enough to hold back the Union ranks.

During the following week, the two sides engaged in a series of skirmishes. For the Union forces, the muggy heat and fierce mosquitoes became as powerful an enemy as the Confederates. Outbreaks of typhoid fever and malaria took more lives than Rebel bullets and weakened the Federal forces.

44

By the end of seven dismal days, the Union had suffered 15,900 casualties—one-seventh of its army. The Confederate losses were also massive; 20,141 men—nearly one-fourth of Lee's army—had been killed, wounded, or captured. The Rebels waited in fear for the final blow from a regrouped Union army.

It never came. Despite losing fewer men, McClellan retreated instead of ordering a counter-attack that could have destroyed Lee's army. Saving Richmond made Lee a Confederate hero, even though the Army of Northern Virginia had been badly weakened.

Longstreet, like Grant out west, proved to be a brutal and determined fighter during the battles. Through his strength and endurance he had gained the admiration of his men, who began calling him, behind his back, by his childhood nickname of "Old Pete."

Lee was elated with Longstreet's performance, and the two men soon became close friends. Lee said that Longstreet is "the Staff of my right hand," and reported to Jefferson Davis that he was "a capital soldier."

At the same time, however, Longstreet had shown himself to be an overly careful strategist. It was becoming clear that Lee and Longstreet had very different ideas about how to wage war. Lee observed, "Longstreet is a good fighter but he is very slow to move."

45

Victory at Second Bull Run

In late July 1862, the Army of Northern Virginia faced another force gathering for an attack on Richmond, this time from north of the city. Union troops were led by General John Pope, an overly confident West Point graduate who had boasted that he would destroy the Rebel army and then pillage the Confederate capital. Lee, who despised Pope for his dishonorable threats, decided on a risky plan to split his army in two—a tactic that had not yet been used in the war.

John Pope led Union troops at Second Bull Run.

Longstreet's force was stationed near Richmond to create the belief among Union scouts that it was the only force defending the capital. Meanwhile, Jackson totally outfoxed Pope in a series of flanking maneuvers, and captured the Union supplies.

Pope, stunned by the Rebels' quick action, was forced to retreat. Pope reorganized his army, however, and moved to attack the Confederates, who were arranged in a defensive position near the old battlefield of Bull Run.

Instead of waiting for the Union advance, Lee wanted to attack on August 29. Longstreet, however, believed that Union reinforcements were on the way and advised caution. Lee took Longstreet's advice and waited anxiously, hoping

46

that his divided troops would be able to ward off the Union attack.

Not until noon of the next day did the Union army advance. In a stroke of luck for the Rebels, the Union army made a concerted attack toward Jackson and ignored the other Rebel position. This concentration of Union men along a narrow front enabled Longstreet to leave his position and move to reinforce Jackson. From there, they launched a fierce counterattack. Once again, Lee, Jackson, and Longstreet dealt a stinging blow to the Union—and sent Pope's army fleeing back to Washington.

Rebel troops soundly defeated the Union army at the Second Bull Run battle.

After the decisive victory at the Second Bull Run, Lee proposed a risky offensive move. This time, he would dare to invade the North, leading his troops across the Potomac and into Maryland. Jackson and Longstreet supported the attack. Like many in the South, they hoped that a resounding victory in Northern territory would convince European nations to recognize the Confederacy as a true nation.

Lee, Jackson, and Longstreet also had other reasons for their invasion. They wanted to distract the Union from Richmond. They also wanted to move the fighting away from the Shenandoah Valley of Virginia during the crucial harvest time.

Longstreet and Jackson disagreed with one element of Lee's plan—they did not want to divide the Army of Northern Virginia as Lee proposed. Up to this point, Lee had shown a unique commanding style—his orders consisted of general suggestions, and he typically allowed his generals to arrange the specific details of a plan. For the invasion into Maryland, however, Lee laid out a clear plan of attack for his generals to follow. Despite Longstreet and Jackson's misgivings, Lee was determined to separate his forces.

Antietam

At his headquarters in southwestern Maryland on September 9, 1862, Lee made four copies of his top-secret battle plan and troop movements. This

48

document was called Special Order 191.
According to the plan, Jackson would
move half of the army west towards
Harpers Ferry, Virginia (now West
Virginia), a small town at the junction of
the Potomac and Shenandoah rivers. There
he would further divide his force and take control
of the Federal armory. Longstreet was to lead the
other half of the army east to Boonsboro, Maryland,
to await further command.

Longstreet realized that the plans had to be
kept secret and ate his copy after he had memorized
its contents. Stonewall Jackson and A.P. Hill were
each given a copy. Union spies stumbled upon a
copy of the plan—wrapped around three cigars—
in a cornfield near an abandoned Rebel camp.
How the plan found its way to that location is
one of the great mysteries of the Civil War, but
it was a blunder that had deadly consequences.

After he learned of Lee's plan, McClellan quickly
began moving his army west from Washington
to meet Longstreet. Meanwhile, Lee—who was
unaware that the enemy knew his plans—called
for more troops to meet at Sharpsburg before
heading to Boonsboro. Sharpsburg, a Maryland
farming community, was divided by Antietam
Creek. The battle that ensued came to be known
among Union troops as Antietam.

On September 15, 1862, when McClellan first
learned of Lee's plans, he had 80,000 men in
place to attack the Rebel army. McClellan was

49

The Battle of Antietam took place on September 17, 1862.

poised to destroy Lee's army, which consisted of only 18,000 men. Instead, McClellan let two crucial days pass. During those days, more of Lee's troops arrived to join Longstreet's defense on the western bank of Antietam Creek. "This is a hard fight and we had better all die than lose it," Longstreet would later say about the battle.

The Rebels knew they faced a severe disadvantage in numbers. "It was easy to see," Longstreet said, "the Confederate army would be cut in two and probably destroyed.... We loaded our little guns with canister and sent a rattle of hail into the Federals as they came up over the crest of the hill."

The fighting began at about 7 A.M. in a cornfield beside a church and raged through most of the day. Federals and Rebels stood at almost point blank range firing until, as one Union officer put it, "the lines melted away like wax in the sun." The death toll was staggering. More than 10,000 men from both sides were dead and wounded by noon.

The horror spread miles away from the battlefield. A nurse described the ghastly scene:

"We went about our work with pale faces and trembling hands... we would catch our breath and listen, and try not to sob, and turn back to the forlorn hospitals, to the suffering at our feet and before our eyes, while the imagination fainted at thought of those other scenes hidden from us beyond the Potomac."

Clara Barton, who later founded the American Red Cross, was a nurse that day in 1862. In one instance she felt her sleeve flutter as she leaned close to a wounded solder to give him a drink of water. She then realized that the flutter had been a bullet that passed through the cloth and killed the man she was tending.

By nightfall, thousands lay drowning in their own blood. There were not enough bandages to go around, so cornhusks were used to cover bullet wounds. The Battle of Antietam became the bloodiest single day in American military history. The Rebels lost 13,700 men and the Union lost 12,350.

At Antietam, although outnumbered and injured, Longstreet fought brilliantly and again showed his fighting spirit as he rode up and down the lines of his men encouraging them with his

On October 1, 1862, President Lincoln took the train to western Maryland to tour the battlefield at Antietam.

51

Confederate soldiers lie dead after the Battle of Antietam. The battle represented the bloodiest single day in American military history.

iron will and fierce bravery. Limping and clad in carpet slippers because of a foot injury, Longstreet showed no signs of pain. His endurance, strength, and persistence seemed beyond the range of any normal man.

His performance was not overlooked by Lee or the other officers. The day had been a bloodbath, and Lee was worried because he had not seen Longstreet return from the battlefield. When Longstreet finally returned to headquarters that night, Lee hugged him. "Ah here he is," Lee affectionately called. "Here comes my war horse from the field he had done so much to save."

The battle was considered a victory for the North, even though they won barely a mile of ground. The Confederate invasion of Union territory, however, was repelled. The Rebel army limped back to Virginia. Confederate survivors of the brutal fight fully expected the Union troops to breathe down their necks at any moment. In fact, if McClellan had moved in, he might have destroyed Lee's army. But the attack never came.

George B. McClellan led Union forces at the Battle of Antietam.

Once again, McClellan had missed an opportunity to destroy the Confederate army—the Rebels had slipped away. If he had acted, McClellan might have ended the war. Instead, he let the Rebels escape to regroup farther south. Lee soon promoted both Longstreet and Jackson to lieutenant general.

In the North, President Lincoln, furious that the Rebels had gotten away, told McClellan, "If you don't want to use the army, I should like to borrow it for a while." Lincoln removed McClellan from his position as commander of the Army of the Potomac. On November 9, 1862, Major General Ambrose E. Burnside took command of the force.

53

A Long-Awaited Opportunity

Despite the internal problems each army faced after Antietam, the Union, at last, had won a major battle. President Lincoln viewed the Union victory as a long-awaited opportunity. In late September he issued the Emancipation Proclamation. According to this order, on January 1, 1863, all slaves in lands under Confederate control were "forever free."

★

Lincoln's Emancipation Proclamation caused an exodus of slaves from the south to the north in 1863.

★

Lincoln's words at that time were mostly symbolic. They did, however, create a strong sense of what the North was fighting for. Although the issue of slavery had always divided the North and the South, the main issue during the first two years of the war had been the Southern states' right to secede. With the Emancipation Proclamation, Lincoln transformed the Civil War into a war for liberty, a fight for the famous principles set down in the Declaration of Independence.

As a result, the Emancipation Proclamation dashed Southern hopes that England or France would enter the war on the side of the Confederacy. Although sympathetic to the Southern cause, both of these countries had outlawed slavery. Now that slavery was the central issue over which the war was being fought, neither of these countries was willing to aid the slaveholding side. The proclamation guaranteed that the war would stay between the North and the South.

54

The irony is that though Lincoln hated slavery, he did not abolish it in the border states that had remained in the Union, such as Maryland and Kentucky. He was a shrewd politician, and did not want to drive Union states into the Confederacy.

Fredericksburg

After McClellan's failure to pursue Lee, Lincoln made it clear that to win the war, the Union army needed to become more aggressive. In addition, the president wanted one resounding victory before the end of year to underline the force of the Emancipation Proclamation. These goals seemed within reach when, immediately after Burnside took command of the Union army, he showed the energy that McClellan had lacked. In a bold campaign, Burnside marched the Army of the Potomac to Fredericksburg, an old Southern city on the banks of the Rappahannock River halfway between Washington, D.C., and Richmond.

Ambrose Burnside replaced George McClellan as commander of the Army of the Potomac.

If he could take Fredericksburg, Burnside reasoned, he would have a clear path to capture the Confederate capital. When Burnside and his huge Army reached the Rappahannock River on

The Emancipation Proclamation

More than a year after the outbreak of the Civil War, Horace Greeley, an outspoken journalist and abolitionist, criticized Lincoln in a *New York Tribune* editorial for not doing enough to end slavery. To this Lincoln replied:

"My paramount object in this struggle is to save the Union, and it is not either to save or destroy slavery. If I could save it by freeing all the slaves I would do it; and if I could do it by freeing some and leaving others alone I would also do that. What I do about Slavery and the colored race, I do because I believe it helps to save the Union."

As the war went on, however, the Union was grief-stricken and confused by what seemed to have become senseless violence. Lincoln knew that he had to bring the meaning of the war to a higher level. The moment had arrived to end slavery.

Even as he had publicly issued the response to Greeley, Lincoln had already begun to draft his Emancipation Proclamation, yet he knew that the success of his plans depended on timing. Although critics condemned him, Lincoln waited. He needed a Union victory to give weight to his proclamation.

With the Battle of Antietam, the Army of the Potomac had forced Lee back to defensive positions, and Lincoln finally had his opportunity. In September 1862, soon after the battle, Lincoln declared that as of January 1, 1863, "All persons held as slaves within any State, or designated part of a State, the people where of shall then be in Rebellion in the United States, shall then, thenceforward, and forever free."

Although the Emancipation Proclamation did not immediately free the slaves—the Rebel states were no longer under control of the Federal government—it ultimately led the way to their freedom.

This fanciful painting depicts Lincoln at work on the Emancipation Proclamation.

November 17, 1863, there were no more than 1,000 Rebels across the river to defend the city. The Army of the Potomac faced a major problem, however. The bridges over the river had been destroyed. In order to cross the river, which was 400 feet wide at Fredericksburg, pontoon bridges would have to be built. As a result, nearly three weeks passed before Burnside's army was ready to cross the Rappahannock.

Meanwhile, as the North became more aggressive, Longstreet grew convinced that the exact opposite strategy—defensive warfare—held the key to Southern victory. In Longstreet's ideal battle, he would secure a position on high ground that created a geographic advantage over the enemy. He would then wait for the enemy to attack, absorb the blow, and wage a devastating counterattack. In the company of Lee and Jackson, whose bold schemes depended on surprising the enemy, Longstreet rarely had a chance to test his approach. The conditions at Fredericksburg gave him that opportunity.

Lee had ordered both Jackson and Longstreet to converge on the city. Jackson's men had marched more than 175 miles in 12 days during cold, rainy weather to reach Fredericksburg. They joined Longstreet's force, who had already begun to dig in.

On the eve of the Union attack, Burnside's men bombarded the city of Fredericksburg to try to weaken the Rebel army. The Union shelling,

James Longstreet

however, did not reach the Confederates. Sheltered from the heavy firing, the Rebels waited across the river—unharmed—for the battle they knew was coming.

The next day, when Burnside's men attempted to cross the Rappahannock, they were met by Rebel snipers. The snipers fired on the Union troops to delay their crossing. And in an area of high ground outside the city, the Confederate army—now 78,000 men strong—secured its position behind a stone wall near the steep slope of Marye's Heights.

Longstreet had carefully chosen the Confederate position next to a sunken road at the base of a group of hills. The sunken road formed a natural trench that was protected by a stone wall.

Confederate forces fire on Union soldiers from their position on Marye's Heights.

On February 24, 1863, the Arizona Territory was formed from part of the New Mexico Territory.

★

Longstreet believed that the trench would protect his army from both enemy fire and the debris of their own artillery. Trenches were not new to warfare. Longstreet, however, improved trenches by adding low walls of dirt that extended from the main trench to protect his men from the deadly shrapnel that whistled through the air during heavy fighting.

In addition to the trenches, Longstreet had arranged artillery pieces so they could rake the open field with crossfire and kill any attackers that the riflemen missed. Within their defensive position, the Rebels awaited the Federals. When Longstreet asked his artillery commander if there should be another gun added to the crossfire, the commander replied, "We cover that ground now so well that we will comb it as with a fine-tooth comb. A chicken could not survive when we open on it!"

Because Union forces had been delayed crossing the river, the attack on Confederate positions outside of town was also set back. This meant that thousands of Union soldiers were left to wander the empty streets of Fredericksburg. Many troops were bored from weeks of waiting to cross the river. Others were on edge from the struggle to fight their way into the city. This mix of emotions led to one of the worst acts of vandalism of the war.

Federal soldiers rampaged through town and stole whatever they could. Homes and businesses were torn apart. Men burned books, paintings, pianos, and other pieces of furniture. Some paraded around town in women's silk clothing before they trampled it in the mud.

At dawn on the day of the battle, thick fog prevented Longstreet from seeing his enemy. As it happened, Burnside's troops first attacked Jackson, south of Longstreet's position. That battle was a give-and-take fight that lasted most of the morning. By about 1 P.M., Federal troops had gathered at the far end of the open field leading up to Marye's Heights. Longstreet made a final check of the lines of his troops lined up behind the stone wall.

Soon bugles sounded as a thick mass of Union soldiers began to move forward in a wave of blue. Rebels watched in amazement as the swarm of soldiers began their double-quick march to Marye's Heights. A Confederate officer, William Miller Owens later recalled:

> *"The enemy, having deployed, now showed himself above the crest of the ridge and advanced in columns of brigades, and at once our guns began their deadly work with shell and solid shot. How beautifully they came on! Their bayonets glistening in the sunlight made the line look a huge serpent of blue and steel."*

The Confederates held their fire until the Union attackers were within range. Then

★

In March 1863, Congress passed the first Conscription Act. This act forced all men between the ages of 20–45 to either join the army, find a substitute, or pay a fee.

★

61

suddenly, and with brutal force, the Rebels began to fire. As the first row of Rebels rose and fired, the Union men fell by the hundreds. The first line stepped back to reload, and a second line of Rebels moved forward and fired. Then Confederate cannons joined the murderous assault, firing canister shot, plow blades, and railroad iron that cut men to pieces. Huge gaps appeared in the enemy lines. A Confederate soldier was awestruck: "We could see our shells bursting in their ranks, making great gaps; but they came on."

Tree branches and shrapnel flew through the air as the Rebels pelted the Yankees, yet the men continued to press onward until it seemed to the Rebels that there was an endless number of men charging Marye's Heights.

From behind the stone wall, the Confederates raced to aim, fire, and reload. It was nearly impossible for them to miss their targets. Relentlessly, Burnside ordered assault after assault. Federal bodies began to pile up three deep on the field. Union soldiers ducked behind dead comrades and tried to return fire. Some soldiers slipped and fell on the blood-soaked grass. Others simply fell and took cover, too frightened to move.

By nightfall, Burnside had ordered seven assaults. Of the thousands of men who marched to the foot of Marye's Heights, only a few made it

Confederate wagons were destroyed and horses were killed during the Battle of Fredericksburg.

within 50 yards of the wall before being killed, injured, captured, or driven back into the woods. Not one Union soldier made it over the stone wall.

Although Longstreet's force had suffered 5,309 casualties, the Rebels had slaughtered the Union army, inflicting more than 12,653 casualties. Longstreet's defensive battle position had proved invincible. In the bitter cold that night, mangled troops in blue covered the blood-soaked field, moaning in agony. Some froze to death. Others were saved when the cold froze their blood and stopped it from flowing out of their wounds. Joshua Chamberlain, a Union officer, lay wounded on the field. He survived by pulling the dead bodies of comrades over him for warmth. At dawn he led troops from the field in retreat.

63

The Battle of Fredericksburg had devastated the North, and morale there hit a new low. On the Southern side, however, there was celebration. Watching the men cheer their easy victory, Lee turned to Longstreet and said, "It is well that war is so terrible, otherwise, we should grow fond of it."

For Longstreet, Fredericksburg had been the perfect battle. He had found his deadly proof that defensive tactics were enough to destroy entire armies. He had pummeled the Union army, without sacrificing huge numbers of his own men.

Lee and Jackson, however, found fault with the battle of Fredericksburg. Although the Confederates had completely crushed the Union army, Burnside's men were able to retreat and escape. Because of their defensive position, the Confederates were not able to deliver a devastating blow—the Union army had fled. Whereas Lee and Jackson were masters of surprising the enemy, Longstreet lacked the flexibility to move from defense to offense on the battlefield.

★

The Idaho Territory was formed in March 1863.

★

Lee and Jackson agreed that more than defensive fighting was needed if the South was going to whip the North. The two men's beliefs were just the opposite of Longstreet's—the Army of Northern Virginia, they were convinced, would win the war by attacking the North when the Yankees least expected it.

The rift between Longstreet's strategies and those of Lee and Jackson was not a major concern

64

in the South in 1862, however. Southerners were elated—the Army of Northern Virginia seemed invincible—and their General Lee was already preparing a bold campaign to invade the North.

Chancellorsville

The year of 1862 was a draining one for Longstreet both at home and on the battlefield. Exhausted by the war, Longstreet rested during the winter months of 1863. After he returned to duty, he was assigned to guard the Richmond area and collect supplies from the local citizens. Taking on this task in his usual determined way, Longstreet had his men gather enough bacon, corn, and feed to supply the entire Army of Northern Virginia and its animals for two months.

Longstreet was busy with this assignment when the battle of Chancellorsville broke out in May 1863. The battle, although a clear Confederate victory, led to one of the Confederacy's greatest losses. In addition to more than 13,000 other casualties, Stonewall Jackson was shot by his own men in the confusion and darkness of the thick woods. He died ten days later.

Lee chose Lieutenant General Richard S. Ewell, a West Point graduate and career soldier, as Jackson's replacement. Ewell, who was nicknamed "Old Baldy," had been injured at the Second Bull Run and had just returned to the army with a new wooden leg. With Jackson's death, the powerful trio of Rebel leaders had been broken.

65

Longstreet did not see action in the Battle of Chancellorsville, shown here, because he was gathering supplies for the Rebel forces.

Gettysburg

After the victory at Chancellorsville, Lee wanted to lead his army into Union territory. Longstreet, however, opposed Lee's plan. The Southern leaders had received word that Grant's army had laid siege to Vicksburg, Mississippi, in the West. Longstreet wanted to take his corps of men west to break the Union siege.

Lee, however, persuaded President Jefferson Davis that a Confederate victory in the North would draw Grant away from the siege. In the end, the Southern leaders chose Lee's plan over Longstreet's. It was the first disagreement between the two men.

By mid-June 1863, the Army of Northern Virginia was marching north, up the Shenandoah

James Longstreet

River Valley into Pennsylvania. The plan was to turn east after crossing the border and move toward Harrisburg, the capital of Pennsylvania.

Lee, as he usually did, used cavalry units under General Jeb Stuart to scout the position of enemy forces. Lee sent Stuart and his men ahead to locate the enemy position. In the past, Stuart's riders had been so superior to Union cavalry that they had literally ridden circles around the Federals and kept Lee well informed. By now, however, Union cavalry under General Alfred Pleasanton had become effective in their own right. Stuart's men ran into fierce battles with Union horsemen, which delayed his report back to Lee. Thus, Lee's huge army—more than 30 miles long on the march—entered Union territory "blind." Lee had no way of knowing that the massive Union force had crossed the Potomac and was moving to cut off the eastward advance of his huge Rebel army.

★

In June 1863, the Battle of Brandy Station, Virginia, marked the first time in the Civil War that Union cavalry matched the Confederate horsemen in skill.

★

As was true of both sides throughout the war, troops took what food and other supplies they needed from the population in any area. Reports came back to Lee's men that there was a shoe factory located in the small nearby farm town of Gettysburg, Pennsylvania. Because the lack of good footwear had plagued the Rebels throughout the war, Lee gave permission for several units to detour into Gettysburg to obtain shoes. There, they encountered a Union

67

The sleepy farming town of Gettysburg, Pennsylvania, became the scene of a fierce three-day battle.

advance party. Suddenly, the sleepy town became an accidental battlefield.

On the first day of the chance encounter, a small Union cavalry brigade held off a much larger Southern force for most of the morning and early afternoon. This success was partially due to the fact that the Union troops were equipped with new breech, or side-loading, rifles. Soldiers using these weapons could fire as many as twenty shots per minute, as opposed to the two or three shots per minute that a skilled rifleman could fire with a front-loading gun. By the time Lee and the rest of the army arrived later that afternoon, however, the Rebels had pushed the Union army back into the rolling hills south of Gettysburg.

Though they had taken heavy losses, the Union army under Fredericksburg veterans General Winfield Scott Hancock and George Meade had secured a strong position from Culp's Hill to Cemetery Ridge. Confident in their defensive position, the Union generals decided to wait for the Rebels to attack first. Lee, in an unusual hesitation, pulled his forces back from attack as night fell on the first day. In later years, military experts believed that had Lee continued the attack on the first day, he might have dislodged the Union troops, who were greatly outnumbered.

Longstreet arrived early on the morning of July 2, 1863. "Look out for work now, boys, for here's the old bulldog again," one soldier yelled as the general passed by. Longstreet had earned a reputation for being demanding. Lee had a similar reputation among his generals. Both men, however, had met with great success, and their troops were tremendously loyal to them.

Lee conveyed his battle plan to Longstreet as the hot July sun rose overhead. Southern scouts knew that after the first day's battle, Union General Dan Sickles and his army held high ground at the Little Round Top and to the north at Cemetery Ridge.

Lee wanted Longstreet to take the two hills known as Little and Big Roundtop. The plan fell apart, however, because the road that Longstreet and his men needed to take was blocked. Although the men broke camp at 9:00 A.M., they did not reach the site of the attack until late in the afternoon.

For four hours the Rebels savagely fought to drive the Union army from their positions. But

69

well-protected Union troops cut down scores of Rebels in places known in Civil War lore—Devil's Den, the Peach Orchard, and finally, Little Round Top. A Confederate officer wrote that as the Rebels charged into brutal Union fire on Little Round Top, "My line wavered like a man trying to walk in a strong wind."

Bloody hand-to-hand fighting ensued. The clash on Little Round Top became one of the most famous battles within the battle. The leader of Union forces was Joshua Chamberlain, who had been wounded at Fredericksburg. After the war, Chamberlain wrote of the vicious battle, "They were close to us, advancing rapidly as they came. We expended our last cartridges. I saw that there was no other way to save the hill or even ourselves, but to charge with the bayonet."

Union troops forced the Rebels back. But the fighting raged back and forth for hours. The Army of Northern Virginia seemed close to victory, when Union reinforcements arrived and further repelled the Rebel assault. Darkness fell on the battlefield, ending the day's fighting. The Round Tops had been held, but the Rebels had come close to success.

When the last Rebel had fallen back, Longstreet said, "I do not hesitate to pronounce this the best...fighting done by any troops on any battle-field." However, he added, "it did not turn out as we had planned."

Rebel forces charged up Little Round Top on the second day of fighting at Gettysburg.

Though his force had fought well, Longstreet had been late to the action due to unforeseen obstacles. In later years, however, his critics accused Longstreet of purposely hesitating because he did not agree with Lee's aggressive plan.

That night, Lee laid out for Longstreet the plan for the next day. Lee ordered Longstreet to send his corps across the open field toward the high ground. Longstreet objected. As he looked toward the distant rise of Cemetery Ridge, he commented, "General, I have been a soldier all my life ... and should know as well as any what a soldier can do ... no fifteen thousand men ever arrayed for battle can take that position."

Lee would not be budged, however. Eventually, he did agree to spare some men who were battered

71

from two days of hard fighting. It fell to Longstreet's old friend George Pickett to lead the futile attack. His troops, who had arrived that morning, were fresh and eager to fight. Pickett himself had never led his men into battle and hungered for glory.

On the morning of July 3, 1863, Longstreet hid his reluctance as he prepared for the charge. He blasted the Union forces with artillery to try to weaken them. He had no way of knowing that the Federal troops, well protected behind a stone wall, were unaffected by the barrage. Finally, he gave Pickett the order to charge.

Years later, Longstreet remembered Pickett gracefully riding into battle. Perfumed hair grazing his shoulders, he shouted, "Up men and to your posts, don't forget today that you are from Old Virginia! Forward!"

As Pickett's men advanced, they were unusually quiet. Because this assault required an approach of nearly a mile before engaging the enemy, the Rebels had been forbidden to give their chilling Rebel yell. The relative quiet did not last long, however.

The Rebels were soon met with the relentless fire of Union cannons, which decimated their lines. Those who were not killed immediately continued to struggle up Cemetery Ridge. "When they were half way up the hill," Longstreet recalled, "the crest of the hill was lit with a solid sheet of flames as the

72

Union forces defeated the Confederates at the Battle of Gettysburg.

masses of infantry rose and fired." As Pickett's men
retreated, Union soldiers taunted them with chants
of "Fredericksburg! Fredericksburg!"

As the defeated men returned to base, an
observer said, "No person could have been more
self-possessed than General Longstreet...I could
now thoroughly appreciate the term Bulldog....
Difficulties seem to make no impression on him
than to make him a little more savage."

"It is all my fault," Lee said to men as they
returned, yet still he believed there was a chance
to defeat the Union army. He ordered Pickett's
men to arrange for a counterattack. "General
Lee," Pickett said, "I have no men."

George Pickett

James Longstreet was a senior at West Point when George Pickett entered the academy in 1842. Pickett had received his appointment to West Point from a young congressman from Illinois. At the time, no one could have predicted that Pickett would go on to lead one of the most famous attacks of the Civil War under reluctant orders from his friend Longstreet. Nor could anyone have known that the young congressman who appointed Pickett, Abraham Lincoln, would become president of the United States.

George Pickett

As a member of the West Point class of 1846, Pickett counted among his classmates the great commander Stonewall Jackson and Union commander George McClellan. When asked to lead the fateful charge at Gettysburg, Pickett, who had graduated last in his class, eagerly accepted. Here, he believed, was his chance for glory. But battlefield glory instead became gory slaughter. Pickett's Charge eventually took its place among the great military blunders of history.

In the years following the war, Southerners blamed Longstreet for the failed charge. Pickett, however, did not hold Longstreet responsible. He had forgiven his friend, but Pickett never forgave Lee. Pickett said of Lee years later, "That old man had my men slaughtered."

When the smoke cleared after the three days of fighting at Gettysburg, more than 51,000 Americans were dead, wounded, or missing. It was the bloodiest battle in American history. It was also the costliest battle in Longstreet's military career.

In 1863, Louisa May Alcott published *Hospital Sketches,* an account of her experiences as a nurse in Union hospitals.

In the years to come, the loss at Gettysburg was considered the battle that lost the war for the Confederacy. And Longstreet would come in for a huge portion of blame because of his tardiness on July 2 and his reluctance on July 3.

Longstreet was not, however, solely responsible for the resounding Rebel defeat at Gettysburg. Jeb Stuart's scouting failure hurt Lee, and Lee himself shared some responsibility. His bold attacks had thrust Rebels into victories that no one thought possible, but at Gettysburg, that boldness led to overconfidence and ultimately to the fall of the Confederate army. Lee offered to resign after Gettysburg, but Jefferson Davis would not permit it. In the minds of Southerners, Lee's reputation remained pure even after the slaughter at Gettysburg. Longstreet, however, would not share the same fate. Eventually, he became the scapegoat for the loss.

After Gettysburg, the Confederate spirit was broken. A wagon train carrying wounded men stretched 17 miles. The pain of the loss was almost unbearable. Lee never again attempted to invade the North.

75

Chapter 5

THE FINAL BATTLES

As devastating as the loss at Gettysburg was, the war was far from over. And Longstreet, though exhausted and discouraged, continued to fight.

Although Longstreet admired Lee, he often lacked confidence in his commander and disagreed with Lee's decisions—especially those that concerned the fighting in the West. Longstreet believed that Lee should draw the fighting to the West to keep the Union army from invading the South. Lee, however, seemed obsessed with protecting his home state of Virginia.

OPPOSITE: The Battle of Chickamauga proved to be Longstreet's finest hour.

At times, Longstreet even tried to leave the Army of Virginia to fight in the West. After Gettysburg, Longstreet wrote to Senator Louis Wigfall, "If I remain here, I fear that we shall go, little at a time, till all will be lost. I hope that I may go west in time to save what there is left of us..." Shortly thereafter, Longstreet was given the chance to fight in the West. He was sent to Chickamauga, Tennessee in September 1863.

Chickamauga

The Battle of Chickamauga was already in progress when Lee bid him farewell. "General," Lee said to Longstreet, "you must beat those people."

Longstreet and his men made military history in early September when they took the train to the battle front in northern Georgia. Because there was no direct rail route, Longstreet's forces rode flatbed cars from Virginia south through the Carolinas to Atlanta. From there they moved northwest to the front. In all they traveled nine days in open cars on 16 different rail lines.

Braxton Bragg led Rebel forces at Chickamauga.

When the company finally arrived in Tennessee, they found that General Braxton Bragg, the commander in charge, had neglected to send a guide to lead them to the Rebel encampments.

Longstreet had to find his way to the battlefield through seven miles of unfamiliar terrain in which enemy capture was a constant risk. It was a bright moonlit night by the time Longstreet reached the woodlands near Chickamauga Creek.

In September 1863, Britain stopped delivery on the "Laird Rams," ships built for the Confederacy.

Longstreet immediately began to look for Bragg, to plan for the next day's assault. Bragg was a gruff man, disliked by most of his men. Longstreet soon learned why Bragg was so unpopular. After the long trip, Longstreet—who needed little sleep himself—learned that Bragg had gone to sleep for the night without having laid out the battle plans for the next day. Longstreet now had to wake the unpleasant general. After a brief meeting, Bragg gave Longstreet command of the left wing of his army, which was 22,000 men strong.

The next morning, on September 19, Longstreet was expected to lead an attack through the completely unfamiliar land. Bragg had divided his army into several divisions that were to attack in a head-on assault, but Bragg's plan was so jumbled that the generals were not sure who and when they were expected to attack. The Rebel army was in complete disarray. The plan was a less organized version of Lee's attack at Gettysburg, and the situation represented everything Longstreet loathed in a military action—disorder and indecision.

The battle broke out in an area of dense woods that camouflaged the Union troops from the

79

Rebels. The battle looked grim for the Rebels. In the thick of the fighting, thinking that Confederate General John Bell Hood had been killed, his second-in-command, General Henry Benning, frantically reported to Longstreet, "General Hood killed, my horse killed, my brigade torn to pieces, and I haven't a single man left." At that moment the battle seemed hopeless. Longstreet smiled and coolly asked Benning if he was certain he could not find one man. Surprised and calmed by Longstreet's confident tone, Benning began to regroup his scattered troops.

The battle continued in what seemed like a hopeless massacre of the Rebel army when suddenly a bulge, or salient, appeared in the enemy line. General William Starke Rosecrans, commander of the Union army and Longstreet's West Point roommate, mistakenly thought there was a gap in the Union line. His attempts to fix that nonexistent gap actually created a real one. The Rebels poured through the weakened part of the Union line to turn the course of the battle into the only great Confederate victory in the West.

In less than 40 minutes, Longstreet's divisions nearly destroyed two Federal divisions. Midway through Longstreet's attack on the area called Snodgrass Ridge, an officer asked Longstreet if the enemy had been beaten. "Yes," Longstreet had replied, yet, "If we had our army of Virginia here, we would have whipped them in half the time."

James Longstreet

Coming after his worst defeat at Gettysburg, this was Longstreet's finest hour—even greater than his victory at Fredericksburg. Longstreet had arrived at Chickamauga to find a disorganized army of hungry, lost, and tired men. He had turned the confusion to a Confederate victory, and earned a new nickname. The men now knew him as the "Bull of the Woods."

★
In October 1863, Ulysses S. Grant replaced General William Rosecrans with General Henry Thomas.
★

Chattanooga

After the battle, Longstreet criticized General Bragg for not pursuing the beaten Union army. The Federals had retreated to the Tennessee city of Chattanooga in September 1863, where Bragg placed them under siege.

Things looked bleak for the Union, until General Ulysses Grant arrived on the scene and took command. Grant had the unusual practice of bringing his wife along with him on military campaigns. She was a calming influence on the Union general and helped to keep him away from whiskey, of which he was quite fond. At the Union camp in Chattanooga, Mrs. Grant heard that her cousin, James Longstreet, was commanding the enemy. Julia Dent Grant said to her husband, "Now Ulysses, you know you are not going to hurt General Longstreet." Grant, however, demonstrated his battlefield grit when he replied, "I will if I can get him; he is in bad company."

81

The Battle of Missionary Ridge was part of the larger Battle of Chattanooga.

There was no need for Julia Grant to worry. The friction between Longstreet and Bragg had gotten Longstreet in trouble with Bragg's close friend, Confederate President Jefferson Davis. Instead of remaining with Bragg on the siege lines, Longstreet was sent to East Tennessee in pursuit of another old enemy, Ambrose Burnside, his foe from Fredericksburg. The Battle of Chattanooga unfolded without Longstreet.

For their siege position, the Rebels had secured a post on a foggy height called Lookout Mountain, which rose 12,000 feet above the Tennessee Valley. Grant and his seconds-in-command, General Joseph Hooker and General William Sherman, devised a surprise attack that entailed scaling the steep mountain and attacking Bragg's men. The next day, under fire, the Union army charged up Lookout Mountain. With fixed bayonets, the men massacred the Rebels. "I have seen men rolling in their own blood. They lay mangled in torn pieces so that even friends could not tell them," one Union soldier wrote.

The Union army's attack caught the Rebels completely off guard, and they captured the mountain in what became known as the "Battle Above the Clouds." The victory forced the Rebels out of Tennessee.

Knoxville

Meanwhile, Longstreet was approaching yet another battle. At Knoxville, in east Tennessee, in December 1863, Longstreet had independent command, a situation in which he was not always comfortable. Longstreet was also forced to lead an attack against a fortified Union position, another situation he disliked. This combination of factors led to a brief battle in which the Rebels were completely massacred, losing 800 men to Burnside's 13. It was almost a complete reversal of Fredericksburg, and Longstreet was forced to retreat.

The Wilderness

After Chickamauga, Lee had written to Longstreet about his campaigns in the East, "I missed you dreadfully...your cheerful face and strong arm

83

would have been invaluable. I hope you will soon
return to me." After his humiliating defeat at
Knoxville, Longstreet did return to Virginia,
crossing the Blue Ridge Mountains in miserable
freezing weather.

Early in 1864, Ulysses Grant was made
commanding general of all Union forces.
Longstreet's friendship with Grant gave him
insight into how he would lead the Union army.
"That man will fight us every day and every hour
till the end of this war," Longstreet warned Lee.
"In order to whip him we must outmaneuver him."

The Battle of the Wilderness was fought in dense woodlands.

By the spring of 1864, Longstreet had rejoined the Army of Northern Virginia in the fifteen miles of dense woodlands and swamp known as the Wilderness. Lee took Longstreet's advice about bringing the fight to Grant. On May 6, 1864, his army launched a surprise attack on the Union left flank. The battle cost Grant close to 18,000 men, compared to Lee's 8,000.

In the past, a Union general might have withdrawn when faced with such losses. Grant, however, lived up to Longstreet's prediction: he never quit. For the first time since the war began, a Union general did not retreat.

Late that night after the first day's battle, Longstreet's veteran force arrived to help establish a defense. Throughout the night, Longstreet directed the trenchwork. Although the Rebels were prepared for the coming fight, the South unexpectedly suffered a major setback.

As Longstreet and generals Micah Jenkins and Joseph Kershaw arranged their men in the thick undergrowth, gunshots rang out. In the dark and the thick brush, nervous Rebels had mistaken the Southern officers for Union attackers. Jenkins was mortally wounded. Two of Kershaw's men were killed instantly. Longstreet was blown several feet from his saddle by a bullet that pierced his throat and exited from his right shoulder. "Friends!" Kershaw shouted to stop the attack. But not before three of his men were dead or mortally wounded.

James Longstreet

The Battle of Spotsylvania continued the fighting begun with the Battle of the Wilderness and featured fierce hand-to-hand fighting.

As a bloody foam spilled from his mouth, Longstreet whispered his orders to his major general, and occasionally lifted his head from where he lay under a tree as a signal to the men that he had not died. Longstreet's men were devastated. One artillery officer later wrote, "I never on any occasion during the four years of the war saw a group of officers and gentlemen more deeply distressed. They were literally bowed down with grief. All of them were in tears. One, by whose side I rode for some distance, was

James Longstreet

himself severely hurt, but he made no allusion to his wound, and I do not believe that he felt it. It was not alone the general they admired who had been shot down—it was, rather, the man they loved."

In 1864, Congress passed the Internal Revenue Act, which increased taxes in order to finance the war.

Incredibly, Longstreet had been shot less than five miles from the spot at which Rebels had mortally wounded Stonewall Jackson a year earlier at Chancellorsville. Now another great Rebel leader was injured. Longstreet lost the use of his right arm for the rest of his life. He could never again raise his voice above a hoarse whisper.

As Longstreet was being carried away in an ambulance, his brigade, unwilling to see another one of their beloved leaders fall, commanded, "Lee to the rear!" They did not want to risk another mistaken shot.

The battle continued over the next two days. Neither side gained much territory and both lost thousands of lives. The Battle of the Wilderness, in May 1864, is perhaps best remembered today for the horror that took place on the second day. Cannon sparks caused the dry undergrowth of the forest to burst into flame. Wounded men trapped in the brush screamed in agony as they were burned alive. So wrenching were the cries that Rebels and Federals alike dropped their weapons and worked side by side to pull any wounded they could from the intense flames. In those terrible hours, the war was forgotten as the soldiers fought to rescue their fellow human beings.

87

"A Thousand Deaths"

Longstreet left the battlefield to recover from his wound. He stayed with his family, which included a new baby son named Robert Lee. "Glad to hear such good accounts of my little namesake," Lee wrote to Longstreet. Lee also wrote to Longstreet that he was eager for him to return to the war. The Rebels were faced with disease and hunger, and were close to defeat.

By the time Longstreet returned to action in October 1864, the war had become a prolonged siege centered in trenches around Richmond. Although the Rebel spirit and courage remained strong, the army was crumbling without bullets, food, or clothing. Men were reduced to eating bark and leaf buds. Defeat was so close that even Lee accepted that his fighting force no longer stood a chance against the huge force of Union soldiers massed around the Confederate capital.

By early spring 1865, the railroad junction at Petersburg, south of Richmond, had fallen into Union hands. By April 4, the Confederate government had fled Richmond by train. Thousands of panicked residents took what belongings they could carry and ran in fear for their lives. The city was in flames. Lee and Longstreet withdrew their forces to an area southwest of Richmond. The plan was to meet up with the forces of General Joseph E. Johnston in North Carolina and continue the fight. But there were just too many Union troops moving too quickly.

On the night of April 7, a group of Lee's men planned to convince their determined general to surrender. The men naturally turned to Longstreet, his friend who had always been a voice of reason and logic. The men believed their advice would carry more weight if it came from Lee's most trusted friend.

If the men expected Longstreet to agree readily, then they must have been shocked by his response. After reminding the men that the penalty for such a suggestion was death, Longstreet said that a retreat was out of the question. "If General Lee doesn't know when to surrender until I tell him," Longstreet had said, "he will never know." Privately, however, Longstreet met with Lee that night to discuss the possibility of surrender. Longstreet assured Lee that his old friend Ulysses Grant would treat the Rebels fairly.

Lee realized that his men were only human. No matter how proud their spirit, their bodies were weak. He had no choice. "Then there is nothing left me but to go and see General Grant, and I would rather die a thousand deaths," Lee said. Indeed, if Lee had not had been brave enough to surrender, the war might have continued for years. Some men among the Southern troops wanted to "scatter like rabbits" and prolong the fight with guerrilla tactics. But Lee had made up his mind. As had been true in battle, so it would be in surrender. There would be no turning back.

89

This engraving depicts Lee's surrender to Grant at Appomattox Court House, Virginia.

On April 9, 1865, Longstreet and his already-legendary commanding general agreed to meet Grant at Appomattox Court House. At every opportunity during the war, Longstreet had challenged Lee's aggressive and bold tactics. Now, as the two men walked into the courthouse on that warm spring day, Longstreet took the offensive. "General," Longstreet said as they walked towards the courthouse, "unless he offers us honorable terms, come back and let us fight it out."

There would be no need to fight it out. Grant's terms of surrender were more generous than anyone could have hoped. The men were stunned—there would be no prison, no parades of captured Confederates down Washington streets. Grant asked the men simply to relinquish their weapons and agree that there would be no more fighting. It was the finest hour of a wretched and wrenching four years.

As Lee left the courthouse, he shook hands with T.J. Goree, the aide who had stayed with Longstreet since they had first met in Texas. "Captain," Lee said, "I am going to put my old War horse under your charge. I want you to take good care of him."

The surrender at Appomattox Court House marked the end of the violent war. But for the nation, it marked the beginning of a political war over a complex dilemma: How would the South be brought back into the Union?

Chapter 6

SOLDIER TO SCALAWAG

The Civil War lasted four years and cost the lives of more than 600,000 Americans. For much of that war, the Confederacy had the upper hand militarily. One reason for Confederate superiority on the battlefield was its trio of masterful commanders. Robert E. Lee, James Longstreet, and Thomas "Stonewall" Jackson were virtual legends, who inspired devotion in their own men and struck fear in the Union forces. Jackson's death only two months before Gettysburg was a terrible blow, but the Rebels believed Lee and Longstreet were more than a match for any of the Union commanders—and they were. In the end, however, the Union's superior resources and larger population won out.

OPPOSITE: Despite his service to the Confederacy, Longstreet was reviled in the South after the Civil War.

The defeat of the South did not in any way lessen the almost religious awe with which Southerners regarded both Lee and the memory of Jackson. Longstreet's reputation, however, suffered greatly after the war. In the years between 1865 and 1900, Longstreet became despised by his wartime comrades and loved by his former enemies.

Soon after the war ended, Longstreet and Grant rekindled their friendship. Grant even wrote a letter to President Andrew Johnson, who had assumed office after Lincoln's assassination in April 1865, pleading with him to grant amnesty, or pardon, to Longstreet. Amnesty would give Longstreet the same rights as other citizens, and he would not be prosecuted for treason. Johnson, however, was not convinced. "There are three persons of the South who can never receive amnesty," the president wrote Longstreet. "Mr. Davis, General Lee, and yourself. You have caused the Union too much trouble."

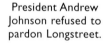

President Andrew Johnson refused to pardon Longstreet.

In many ways, it is not surprising that Johnson denied Longstreet a pardon. For four years the Confederates had fought to tear their states away from the Union. Now politicians in the North were determined to bring the South back into the Union on Northern terms. "The strongest laws are those established by the sword.... The decision was in favor of the North, so that her construction becomes law, and should be accepted," Johnson stated in one speech.

For their part, Southerners were defeated, but their spirit remained defiant. The fact that much of the South lay in ruins only magnified the bitterness they felt toward the North. Few Southerners, except free African Americans, were eager to cooperate with Union efforts in the so-called Reconstruction. To win the people of the South over to the cause of Reconstruction, congressional leaders asked Confederate soldiers to advise the people that the Reconstruction plans were in their best interest.

★

In May 1865, President Andrew Johnson declared that only those who agreed to take a loyalty oath could hold office.

★

One of the few Confederates who agreed with the Northern point of view was Longstreet. After he wrote a letter to the editor of a local newspaper urging Southerners to cooperate with the North, Longstreet showed his draft to his uncle Augustus. "It will ruin you, son, if you publish it," Augustus warned.

In the letter, Longstreet wrote that Southern states should follow decisions made by the U.S. Congress. "We are a conquered people... but one course is left... to accept the terms offered by the conquerors," he wrote. Even worse in the eyes of many white Southerners, Longstreet also wrote in support of the voting rights of former slaves.

95

★

On Christmas Day 1868, Andrew Johnson pardoned all remaining Confederates.

★

"His vote, with the vote that will go with him," Longstreet wrote, "will hold to his rights."

Augustus Longstreet's prediction proved correct. Longstreet later wrote, "The afternoon of the day upon which my letter was published the paper that had called for advice published a column of editorial calling me a traitor! Deserter of my friends! And accusing me of joining the enemy!"

Newspaper editors were not the only ones who jeered Longstreet. Longstreet's friends began to ignore him, and even passed him on the street without speaking. The business he had started at a cotton warehouse in New Orleans began to fail. Within a few weeks, Longstreet was out of a job.

But the letter was not the only problem for Longstreet. Soon after the war, he became a Republican. At that time, a group called the Radical Republicans had great power in Congress. These men insisted on punishing the South by breaking it into military districts governed by Union officers and controlled by Union troops. Longstreet felt that the best way to get the military out of the South was to join the dominant party and work for change. But by joining the party of Abraham Lincoln, he sealed his reputation as a villain among Southerners.

In a few short years, Longstreet sank from being viewed simply as a traitor to being blamed as the major cause that the South lost the war.

The Battle of Liberty Place

When he took office as president in 1869, Ulysses Grant was faced with widespread violence against African Americans and Republican officials in the South. Grant, however, did little to stop white violence, because he felt it was too dangerous to have Federal troops step between whites and blacks in the South. The hands-off policy enabled a racist vigilante group, the White League, to form in Louisiana in 1874. The purpose of this group was to establish a "white man's government" and put down the "insolent African."

In September 1874, more than 3,500 members of the White League gathered in New Orleans to demand the Northern governor of the state resign. The governor, fearing violence, called out 3,600 police officers and black militia. Their commander was James Longstreet—customs surveyor and a former Confederate general. The officers and militia formed a ring around the Customs House where the governor and his staff had taken shelter. But the White Leaguers charged, captured Longstreet, and forced the governor to flee. The violence left more than 100 men killed and wounded, the worst street riot in American history.

Three days later, Grant sent Federal troops to New Orleans, and the White Leaguers vanished. But Southern hatred for Longstreet reached even greater levels when word spread that he had led black troops against whites. "It was with great difficulty," said one White League officer, "that I prevented the men from firing at Longstreet."

In many ways, it probably hurt Longstreet that Lee died only five years after the war's end. Like Longstreet, Lee advised Southerners to accept defeat and adapt to a changed way of life. And although Lee and Longstreet had disagreements about battle strategy, Lee never criticized Longstreet after the war. The fact that he was not alive to defend his battlefield "war horse" was unfortunate for Longstreet.

On the other hand, with Grant's election as president in 1868, Longstreet's professional opportunities for government service were great. Grant first appointed Longstreet the surveyor of customs for the Port of New Orleans. From that point until the end of his life, Longstreet served in various minor posts.

Though he was financially secure from 1870 on, Longstreet became one of the most vilified men in the South over the next thirty years. In newspapers throughout the South, he was called a "scalawag," the insulting name given to a Southerner who cooperated with the Northern authorities. Soon after Longstreet's role in the Battle of Liberty Place became widely known, Southern writers—led by former Confederate general Jubal A. Early—began a campaign

Confederate general Jubal A. Early blamed Longstreet for the South's defeat.

to make anyone in the South who did not already despise Lee's "Old War Horse" blame him for the Confederate defeat.

The main evidence against Longstreet was that he had been late to the battle on the second day at Gettysburg, and that he had argued with Lee about Pickett's Charge. If Longstreet had obeyed orders, these critics claimed, the battle would have turned out differently. Perhaps the Rebels would have won the battle—and even the entire war.

Longstreet spent the remaining years of his life defending his reputation and justifying his wartime conduct. He wrote numerous accounts of the war in which he sometimes criticized Lee's strategies. Eventually he began to publicly criticize Lee and claim that he had been the brains behind Lee's success. Rather than restoring Longstreet's reputation, these claims further enraged his critics.

For the rest of his life, Longstreet suffered from the pain of the gunshot wound to the throat that he received at the Battle of the Wilderness. In his later years, he lost the sight in one eye and became almost totally deaf. In 1889, Longstreet's wife of more than forty years, Maria Louise, died. Nine years later, the 76-year-old Longstreet married 34-year-old Helen Dortsch.

By the beginning of the twentieth century, most men who had fought and survived the Civil War were dead. Lee had died of stroke in 1870. Grant had served two

★

In 1885, the Washington Monument was dedicated after 36 years of construction.

★

99

terms as president before dying of throat cancer in 1885. The Old South had disappeared, and the only general left to bear the burden of the loss was "Old Pete." In other circumstances, this might have been a time of great honor for the man who had been in more major battles than either Lee or Jackson. Instead, however, Longstreet was persecuted by his old comrades—the land he risked his life to liberate never forgave him. After his death on January 2, 1904, Helen wrote a biography of her husband that included a foreword from an unlikely source—Dan Sickles, the general who had battled Longstreet years before at Gettysburg.

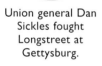

Union general Dan Sickles fought Longstreet at Gettysburg.

"Farewell, Longstreet!" Sickles wrote. "I shall follow you very soon. May we meet in the happy realm where strife is unknown and friendship is eternal!"

Though he fought from Bull Run to Appomattox, "Old Pete" commanded little respect at his death. Only as the twentieth century came to an end did Civil War historians put James A. Longstreet back in his rightful place among the great leaders of the Civil War.

Glossary

amnesty A pardon by the government.

armory A place where military equipment is stored.

artillery Large weapons used by fighting forces that fall into three categories—guns, cannons, and mortars.

brigade A military unit smaller than a division, usually consisting of three to five regiments of 500 to 1,000 soldiers.

cholera A severe intestinal disease.

emancipation Freedom.

epaulet A fringed shoulder pad worn as part of a military uniform.

nullification The attempt of a state to prevent enforcement of a federal law within its boundaries.

pontoon A flat-bottomed boat.

regiment A military unit smaller than a brigade or division.

secede To break away.

scapegoat One that bears the blame for others.

skirmish Minor or preliminary conflicts or disputes.

trench A ditch used for military defense.

For More Information

Books

Gaines, Ann Graham. *The Confederacy and the Civil War in American History*. Berkeley Heights, NJ: Enslow Publishers, 2000.

Green, Carl M. and Sanford, William. *Confederate Generals of the Civil War*. Berkeley Heights, NJ: Enslow Publishers, 1998.

Harmon, Dan, Meier, Arthur, and Schlesinger. *Civil War Generals*. Broomall, PA: Chelsea House Publishers, 1998.

Yancey, Diane. *Leaders of the North and South: Civil War*. San Diego: Lucent Books, 2000.

Web Sites

http://www.civilwarhome.com/longbio.htm

A web page dedicated to the biography of General James Longstreet.

http://www.wtj.com/archives/longstreet

Read General Longstreet's memoirs online, detailing his battle plans and reactions to the Civil War.

Index

103